Fordington Remembered

Growing up in and around Dorchester

Fordington Remembered

Growing up in and around Dorchester

David J. Forrester

Roving
Press

© 2014 David J. Forrester

Published by Roving Press Ltd
4 Southover Cottages, Frampton, Dorset, DT2 9NQ, UK
Tel: +44 (0)1300 321531, www.rovingpress.co.uk

First published 2014 by Roving Press Ltd

ISBN: 978-1-906651-237

British Library Cataloguing in Publication Data
A catalogue record for this book is available from the British Library

Front cover illustration courtesy of Mill Street Housing Society.

Set in 11.5/13 pt Minion by Beamreach Printing (www.beamreachuk.co.uk)
Printed and bound by Henry Ling Ltd, at the Dorset Press, Dorchester, DT1 1HD

This book is dedicated to
David, Derek and Mick, three lifelong friends,
and also my loving wife Roselyn.

Friends Mick Croft, Derek Pride, David Forrester and David Moxom

Author royalties from this book are shared between the Rotary Foundation and Dorset ME Support Group.

Contents

(Copyright Mill Street Housing Society.)

Foreword

One of the benefits of our greatly developed means of communication in the last thirty years has been the encouragement of the writing of memoirs. Before word-processing and computers it was always laborious and off-putting to write, type and publish one's own work, not least because it required a wide readership to make it financially viable. Now we can all do it and the result has been an enormously valuable addition to social history.

David Forrester's recollections of mid-20th century Fordington are a splendid example of what can be done. The life of boys in a not-very-advantaged part of Dorchester is vividly described, with imagery, wonder and compassion.

Fordington is now respectable, pleasant, even a little dull perhaps. David lived there at the tail-end of a much more turbulent time in history, in which the name of the village became a byword for deprivation, disease and criminality among the middle-classes of flourishing Dorchester.

The point was that Fordington was not part of the county town, and for most of its history was outside the jurisdiction of the municipal authorities. The actual authority was not legally clear, in a confusion of feudal rights and, inevitably, when opportunity for misbehaviour appeared, advantage was taken. To some extent, Fordington had always provided an out-of-town refuge for the fringe of the Dorchester community, but the agricultural developments of the 19th century vastly increased the population of footloose and unsettled people. It was the use of gang-labour in the great farming surge of the 19th century that created the need for a pool of unattached farm-workers. The cottages poorly built for the crowds soon became festering slums and hovels, particularly in the area around the mill.

It was not until the scandal and tragedy of the 1854 cholera epidemic that notice was taken of the situation, and progress was slow for the next hundred years. In the early 20th century policemen would still only venture in twos along Mill Street. As David found, echoes of suspicion still remained among Dorchester people long after the village was quiet and well behaved.

I enjoyed Dave's memoirs immensely and heartily recommend the book as a valuable addition to our social history and as a jolly good read.

Terry Hearing
Local author, historian and Rotarian

Preface

Standing in my daughter's home in St Neots, Cambridgeshire, I watched the children return from school, coats thrown down; they rushed to be first on the computer to play football or some other computer game. This is their world, staring at one of a choice of screens they seem to have. Shiny new bikes stand outside virtually unused, while a friend waits at another screen somewhere across town or maybe in another place altogether – it doesn't really matter, you can play with anyone anywhere in the world.

Don't get me wrong, they are not all couch potatoes; one of our granddaughters is a junior world champion rower now studying at Oxford, and the youngest is a promising footballer always keen to tell us how many goals he has scored. However, on the whole, their lives are so different from that experienced by us Fordington boys in the 1940s and '50s that I felt a need to put it down in writing, to let others know; in a way it is a piece of social history that I felt needed recording, just as their world is recorded daily on Facebook or Twitter.

Acknowledgements

Without the help of family, friends and acquaintances, this book would not have been possible and I would like to thank the following: wife Ros, who had to suffer my moods as things went wrong and encouraged me to continue; Julie and Tim Musk of Roving Press for their help and encouragement; my brother Brian for some of the photos and loan of the cigarette box I made; Les Philips, a friend I first met in Mr Tucker's forge as an apprentice when I was at the Boys' School, for the loan of photos; Terry Hearing, local historian, fellow Rotarian and friend; Pauline Camm, always ready to help sort out my mistakes; Rupert Edwards and Judith Dearlove, so helpful with information and pictures of old Mill Street; David Greenwood for giving his time in sorting archives; Alan Rodgers, an apprentice at Lott & Walne in the 1950s, for his photos; Margaret Wellesley-Miller who helped me trace Alan; David Moxom, for nearly 70 years of friendship and help in my research; Derek Pride who pointed me in the right direction on several occasions; Brian Bates who helped trace information; Sally Wales and Dorset County Council for information and photos of Carey Camp; Helen Curtis, Keith Kellaway and Melvin Cross, who gave me access to pictures of the Magpies; Don Ireland for help in finding 'the Croucher's' grave; Valerie Dicker and George Wickham, for providing photos from the Dorset County Museum.

(Following pages) Aerial photograph of lower High Street Fordington and London Road. (Courtesy of Dorset County Museum.)

The war years

My story begins in Forest Hill, London, a strange start for someone who prides himself on being a Dorset man. The date was 1 May 1943. The war was raging all about us and London was suffering more than most. My father Charles, a Londoner from the Queens Road, West Ham (a lifelong 'Hammers' supporter), was in the RAF, seconded to the Rover factory in Birmingham, testing aircraft engines. My mother Winifred, who was born in Somerset and not a Londoner, was not enjoying the Blitz. After leaving hospital we were bombed out of the house in an unexpected raid and the ceiling fell in on my cot. At this time my 8-year-old brother Brian was already suffering from St Vitus Dance, brought about by the constant bombing.

My mother's mind was made up, and when I was 3 months old we decamped to Piddlehinton. What bliss was the silence of the Piddle Valley in July – birds singing and no bombs. My brother attended the local school and mother enjoyed life once more, living with her aunt Emma Damon. She was able to bring us up in the rural peace of Piddlehinton, where most things were available, even in wartime. After a while we returned to London, but soon another near miss ensured that we moved back to the Piddle Valley until the end of the war.

As in many houses at that time, cooking facilities were limited to a range (forerunner of the Aga or Rayburn) and two paraffin stoves. The outside toilet facilities were rustic, set in part of the lean-to outhouse; the door being six inches off the floor and open at the top, the place could be a little draughty. There was a large flat wooden box with a door on the front, a hole in the top for a seat and a bucket underneath. The paper was cut squares of newspaper threaded on a piece of string, which hung on a rusty nail at the side. As the days went by before the toilet was emptied you began to realise it was good to have air flow under the door. The bucket was emptied by the gardener; he tipped it into a trench dug across the garden. At the right time of year runner beans were planted in the filled-in trench. Aunt Emma grew the best beans you have ever seen.

When peace came my father, now demobbed from the RAF, visited and attempted to make plans for a move back to London. My mother was having none of this and persuaded him that our future lay in Dorset and we moved to Dorchester. But this was not the end of our attachment to Piddlehinton. I visited many times as a boy. Feeding the ducks on the river over the wall at the end of the garden was one of my favourite pastimes.

3

A new start: Forrester's Stores

My mother (née Randall) had cousins in Dorchester. At this time they owned several properties, one of them a greengrocer's at No. 33 High Street, Fordington, together with the house next door, No. 35. My parents arranged to rent these properties, little knowing at that time that this would keep them in Dorchester for the rest of their lives. I was now 3 years old and my first memory is of us sitting in the dark awaiting the furniture van's arrival. When it did we moved in and it was goodbye London!

Mother took over the shop with the name Forrester's proudly displayed over the door, where it stayed for some 35 years. This shop in the 'Open All Hours' tradition sold everything from cotton reels to cauliflowers. In the beginning things were tough, partly because the previous tenant had taken the rationing stamps with which my mother could order new supplies. To make matters worse, some of the boxes on the shelves around the back that should have been full of supplies were actually empty.

My mother outside Forrester's Stores and our home at No. 35.

The shop and house were linked, the house being uphill from the shop, the latter entered through a private doorway and down three steps. The shop front door was fitted with a bell which rang when someone entered. Mother, if preparing dinner or carrying out some other household task, would then enter the shop, down the steps, to serve a customer. Often in years past, I have wondered how many thousands of times my mother walked down those steps. No wonder she kept fit.

Outside the vegetables were displayed on two long benches. My father would write on the window in shoe-white things like 'Sprouts 2d a pound'. In the windows other goods were on show – fruit such as apples, oranges and later the much sought-after banana (in the early days mum had a list of those wanting bananas and when they came in she had to ration them), bread, rolls, cakes and Wagon Wheels. These I remember were one of the first things you could buy and send off the wrapper for gifts. There were also Bridgewater Wafers, the first ever chocolate wafer biscuit wrapped in silver and blue foil.

As you entered the shop you faced a large hardwood counter. In front was a row of sacks, the tops neatly rolled down to reveal dried peas, lentils (both red and green), butter beans, split peas, pearl barley and haricot beans. On two occasions a young child (not the same one) picked a pea out of the sack and pushed it up his nose. Failure in all efforts to remove this pea led both times to the child being taken to hospital to have the offending item removed. Later as the dried goods went out of fashion, these sacks were replaced by boxes containing bottles of Corona fizzy drinks. These came in wonderful flavours such as Ice Cream Soda and Dandelion and Burdock and for us these drinks were pure nectar.

On each side of the counter stood a pair of scales, a small set for weighing sweets and sherbet and a larger pair for cheese and ham. Behind the counter was another even larger scale with black weights stacked at the side: all dry goods were sold by weight. At the side on a marble slab there was always a large Cheddar cheese and ham on the bone. Both were hand cut and weighed according to need.

To the left of the counter at the front stood a large glass cabinet. This held a myriad of things: cottons and needles, birthday cards, gas mantles, tap washers, menders for pots or watering cans with holes in, fuse wire, hair nets, even knicker elastic, it was all there somewhere. To the right were jars and boxes of sweets, chews and sherbet. Sweets were in short supply at first and of course rationed. However, as the years passed the choice became much wider, which meant my mother wasted even more time waiting for children to choose how they would spend their 2d.

Along both sides of the shop at the front were shelves stacked with tinned goods, much used in those early days. Another shelf held mother's homemade pickles. At the rear were breakfast cereals such as Cornflakes, Shredded Wheat, Weetabix and porridge (a very poor range by today's standards), washing powders and soap flakes with good old names like Surf, Oxydol, Tide and Lux Flakes. The toilet soap was also of limited choice – Lifebuoy (very smelly), Palmolive and Lux. Washing soap came in three colours – red, green and yellow (was there really any difference?). They arrived at the shop in wooden crates, as did many of the supplies at that time. When opened, these strong-smelling boxes revealed their contents: long rough-cut blocks perhaps 3 inches square by 2 ft long. These soaps were sold by weight; the required amount was cut with a knife and placed on a piece of newspaper on the scales at the rear of the counter. This set of scales was also used for weighing potatoes and other vegetables. As I grew older I earned pocket money by chopping up all the wooden delivery boxes to make bundles of kindling. There was quite a market for this as everyone

Some of the old brands on display.

had open fires, boilers or ranges to light. Gradually the wood was replaced by cardboard, so the kindling disappeared, to be replaced by firelighters.

Behind the counter to the left stood a barrel of malt vinegar and this was measured out into various containers brought in by the customer. The amount required was measured using pewter mugs stamped and marked with quarter pint, half pint and pint. The Weights and Measures Inspector, who always arrived unannounced, checked these measuring mugs and also the scales regularly.

Once a year in October a glass cabinet was brought into use to display the fireworks, and this was greeted with great excitement. Boys stood for ages looking at Little Demons, Thunder Flashes, Roman Candles, Silver Rain, Golden Rain and Mount Etna, to name a few. The interesting fact about this was not revealed to me until later in life, when someone said that mother was one of the few shops in town with a gunpowder licence. This allowed her to sell fireworks, which explains now why so many strangers visited the shop during October.

Lighting was provided by three gas lamps set in globes hanging one in each window and one above the counter. How I loved the dark evenings when I was allowed to take the pole with a hook on it and pull on the silver ring, sending the light popping into life. There was something warm and comforting as the gas hissed and bubbled, an experience that cannot be equalled with a 60W bulb.

In the 1940s and early 1950s Fordington was a relatively poor area, especially Mill Street. Children would often visit the shop and ask for a 'penny apple' (one old penny). As time passed, finding an apple for a penny

Copyright Mill Street Housing Society.

became more difficult. It was clear that many times my mother dispensed apples for a penny out of the goodness of her heart. Another favourite with the children was a penny Oxo cube (beef stock cube). Having purchased the Oxo children would nibble and suck them for hours, often sharing with a couple of others. It is hard to imagine a child doing this now, but at the time it was very common. I have often wondered since whether their enjoyment of these was perhaps due to their very poor diet. I believe they unknowingly were fulfilling a need, much in the way that cattle seek out and lick mineral blocks in a field. These Oxo cubes came to mother in a small tin, and mum had a list of people waiting for these tins, which the men used as sandwich boxes (no Tupperware yet).

In those hard days, it was not uncommon for a woman with two children to buy one faggot which she would cook with gravy. Her husband would have half, the children a quarter each and she would have the gravy and mashed potato. In those days also dinner was often served with a large chunk of bread to make it go around. Bread and cheese were the two cheap staple foods on which many working men lived. In fact my father, who was brought up in the East End of London, always had a chunk of bread with his dinner and drank a mug of water the greens had been cooked in. 'That's where all the goodness is,' he would say, though having tried it once, I was never convinced.

Much more appetising was sherbet, a great children's favourite, and 2d worth of this served up in a triangular-shaped bag went a long way. A bag would be shared with several others, all of whom licked their finger before plunging it into the bag, so that the yellow sherbet stuck to the finger when it was withdrawn and the sherbet was sucked off. Little wonder that bugs travelled so fast in those times. All of those who had shared the sherbet could be recognised instantly by their bright yellow forefingers, which stayed this way for several hours. No concerns about E numbers in those days.

As I have said, times were hard and money was always short in Fordington. Trusted customers were allowed to put purchases 'on the slate' and they would settle this bill later, or in some cases never. Others would pay into the Christmas Club; each one would have a little book, kept by my mother, and each week or whenever they could afford it they would give my mother a few pence, which would be put into the tin with the updated book. At Christmas this would allow them to afford the luxury things that we now take for granted and consume in our normal daily diet, such as tinned fruit, fizzy drinks, bananas, mandarins and nuts.

If anything happened in the village news spread at the speed of light. Great excitement was caused one day, which gathered us lads from all over Fordington. The baker was delivering bread and cakes to my mother and his mode of transport was a wonderful old bread van pulled by a lovely Shire horse. The horse, as with all working horses, knew its way around town as well as any of us. He was never tied up but waited patiently at every stop while the bread man delivered his wonderful wares. On this sad occasion, however, something frightened the horse and he bolted. With his heavy cart behind him he galloped a short distance down the hill, lost control and with the weight of the cart pushing him on, smashed through the wall and ended up with his head and front legs through No. 21 High Street, ruining the bay window. One of the shafts of the van shattered and stuck into him. The poor beast was put down where he had stopped, and many of the children were quickly hurried away by parents when they realised what was going on. The window was mended and wall rebuilt, and though it was over 50 years ago, you can still see the replacement wall in a different colour outside No. 21, bearing testimony to this event.

Mr Les Frost of Great Western Road with the last working horse in Dorchester. Les delivered to customers of James Foot Ltd, a local corn and seed merchant, who had chickens in their backyard. (Courtesy of Les Philips.)

As people look at this wall today I suspect that few know the tale of why this section differs from the rest.

Equally exciting were the times when sheep and cattle were driven through town. On one memorable day, two of the horned bullocks broke away from the rest and entered Dyers, the grocers at the bottom of High East Street. They went through the shop and into the passage behind. From here it was a great struggle to turn them around and get them out through the shop and back into the street. It is difficult for the reader to picture the

Steers leaving Dyers in 1954. (Courtesy of Michael and Polly Legg.)

mess in the shop that this incident caused, as many goods were stacked on the floor. For some time after we would open the door to Dyers and make loud mooing noises, which somehow never amused Mr Rosendale, the shop owner.

The day's takings from mum's shop went into the cash box, and after the shop closed I would often be asked to add the money up. When I had finished, mother would check the piles of coins and enter the amount into her cash book. It shows how things have changed; I would say something like 'Twelve pounds, 9 shillings and 10 pence', and mother would say 'Oh, quite a good day today'. Sometimes on a Saturday it may have been as much as £15. It sounds ridiculous now.

Mother's shop was open from 8 am until 6 pm Monday to Saturday, with an hour for dinner. Early closing was on Wednesday, which allowed my mother to go to town and shop herself. The rest of the shops in town closed on Thursday afternoons. Of course the shop never really closed, and out of hours there was often a knock on the door; one of the regulars had forgotten one thing or another, but my mother was always patient and provided what was required. Knocks on the door were regular for another reason: we were the only family with a telephone in those days. People would come and ask to use the phone for many reasons, mostly emergencies and families with problems: we always knew what was going on. When someone was ill, mother called the doctor or father went to see what was wrong – not that he had any medical skills. On two occasions I remember women called at the shop for my father who, after a visit to their home, sadly told them that their husbands had passed away. Everyone in Fordington knew everybody else and help was never far away. How different things are now, when people hardly know their next-door neighbours. When mother went to town she never locked the front door, and neither did anyone in the street, until later in the 1960s when things began to change.

One thing that amused me as a boy was the way some women came into the shop. They always seemed to have their hair in curlers, and this was covered with a scarf done up into a kind of turban. Out of the corners of their mouths a cigarette dangled complete with an inch-long piece of ash, which never seemed to fall off. The amazing thing about it was that they managed to order their goods and carry out a conversation while the cigarette dangled and bobbed up and down, the ash always threatening to fall but never quite doing so.

As a lad one of my chores was to stack fresh goods on the shelf. My favourite job was to deliver boxes of groceries that had been ordered. Although I was not paid for running these errands, I was always in with a chance of a penny or two or some sweets when I made the delivery.

At the weekend we sometimes had a bonfire to get rid of packaging; this became more regular as cardboard replaced wooden boxes. On one occasion a tin of baked beans must have fallen into the rubbish box and consequently ended up in the fire. As we stood watching there was a huge bang and the back of the house, windows and those watching were sprayed with warm beans. This incident was mentioned for years after, whenever we had a bonfire.

Once the shop was established it did reasonably well. At the time, prices were fixed for all outlets and published in *The Grocer*, the shopkeeper's bible. This being so, you couldn't go to town and buy things cheaper in another shop. Once this restriction was lifted and supermarkets arrived, with the inevitable price competition, things became more difficult. This competition eventually killed off many of the old Dorchester stores. I can call to mind Dyers, Boons, County Stores, Fares Stores and Parsons, all well-established grocers who eventually fell by the wayside. Parsons was the first shop to use a gimmick to encourage customers in and buy coffee. Being forward thinking, they fixed a grill at the side of the coffee roaster with a fan that blew the wonderful smell of coffee out into the High Street – very hard to resist. Over

the years there were many rumours that Parsons was to close. When her husband Jack, later to become Mayor, went off to war, Mrs Vera Parsons kept the shop going with help from her mother-in-law and sister-in-law. After the death of her husband she ran the shop for some 40 years. Mrs Parsons sold it on the basis that it would continue in the same vein. Eventually the business closed and it is now two shops, Empire Kebabs and China Express. I wonder what Vera would make of that?

Parsons in High East Street. (Courtesy of Dorset County Museum.)

The newspaper headline of 29 September 1982 read 'County town's oldest shop changes hands after 111 years. Parsons, still sending out exquisite smells of roasting coffee into the streets of Dorchester'. (Source: Dorset Echo, Dorset History Centre.)

Finally with the onset of decimalisation in 1971, my mother called it a day and our shop closed. Even when the shop was doing quite well it could never really keep us, so Dad always had at least one other job and sometimes as many as three. He worked for many years as a boiler man for the army, served silver service at the Kings Arms Hotel in High East Street (those were the days), and at weekends he also did painting and decorating for George Cake, a local builder. I think that often as children we didn't realise how difficult things were for our parents in those years after the war.

Lott & Walne

Lott & Walne's business at the bottom of High Street Fordington started in the 1830s and was a big local employer. The works bell was used by many living in Fordington as their time keeper, ringing at the start of work at 8 o'clock, with 12.30 for lunch (or dinner, as it was in those days the main meal, always taken at this time), and 5 o'clock signalling the end of the working day. The foundry produced farm implements, pumps and manhole covers, some still seen around Dorchester today, and many bespoke pieces of

Lott & Walne in its hey-day. (Photos courtesy of T. Hearing (top) and Alan Rodgers (bottom).)

equipment, especially as the foundry contained a large blacksmith's shop. As boys we often went down to see what was going on. The large double doors at the end of the casting shop had slits worn in them. This enabled us to peep through and see the red-hot metal being poured into the sand moulds laid out on the floor – very exciting. At the front of the building on the first floor a wooden flap was hinged out and deliveries of goods were pulled up to the store by crane. Can you imagine any firm being allowed to lift heavy objects swinging on a crane over a public footpath today?

Over the years L&W found competing with large companies more and more difficult and by 1967 had stopped casting. Despite changing their range of goods and selling bought-in farm machinery such as bailers, hay turners and

L&W provided farmers with anything they wanted and many tools were produced to fulfil a special need. They also produced the basics, such as this horse-drawn plough (on display in St George's Church).

seed drills, eventually the company closed in 1987 and the work bell rang no more. The building has now been put to further use as flats.

St George's Infants School

In 1946 one could start school at the age of three, and the infants school of St George's was at the top of the High Street. I remember the first morning, as my mother left me screaming in the hands of the teacher. After a while I settled down to enjoy the company of other children. It was here that I saw across the room David Moxom; he was 2 years older and lived around the corner. We were destined to become lifelong friends.

The school was based on one huge room with dividers that could be drawn across to create several classrooms. The headmistress Miss Parsons (nobody's favourite) was a jolly soul, who appeared to get great joy out of punishing you with a thick wooden pointer. On one occasion a school inspector visited us and asked if she ever hit us. I stupidly stood up and said yes, whereupon he asked me to show him where the weapon was kept. Needless to say it wasn't there; however, she soon found and used it when he had gone. What memories! Another teacher, Miss Palmer, was much more humane and more to my liking. Do boys really fall in love at age four or five?

When we first joined the school things were easy-going, learning through

St George's Infants School circa 1976. (Courtesy of Dorset County Museum.)

play. After lunch, fold-up camp beds were retrieved from the cupboard and put up. We were all made to have an afternoon nap; no wonder I still enjoy one now. The school was well situated, with Salisbury Fields only a short distance away through the passageway at the top of the road. The field was ideal for running around on dry days; when too wet, the playground was used. The toilets were basic, consisting of a corrugated-iron roofed 'lean-to' with a length of guttering to carry the urine. There were no doors, just an open gap on the side, so in winter you didn't stay long.

School Court, the site of the school, now built over – all that remains is the passage we used to enter the school.

St George's Day on Fordington Green. Headmistress Miss Parsons, glasses and hair in a bun as always. Behind her is Miss Palmer, my favourite teacher.

Fordington infants, circa 1947. Twins Keith and Gladys Basket (front row far right) and me (front centre).

One of my happy memories of the school was the number of musical instruments we had. There was what seemed to be a huge array of percussion instruments, which we could ring, tap, bang and shake. How I loved making a noise, but was it music? Who cares! It made one come alive. As you get older you appreciate the 'sound of silence'!

Sunday School

You may wonder why a young lad would enjoy going to school on a Sunday, but we loved it; and unlike now, there was little else to do. So, although we were at the school Monday to Friday, many of us also attended Sunday school. This was held in the Moule Institute which stood at the top of the High Street near the school. How sad that these days Sunday is just another day of the week and Sunday schools are few and far between. When I look back we had none of today's distractions.

For children who rarely went anywhere far from Dorchester, the Sunday school outing was the highlight of the year. We would all get on the coach,

The Moule Institute or Memorial Coffee Tavern, much used for Sunday school and youth club. (Courtesy of Alan Rodgers.)

picnic in hand, rushing to get the back seat, and would be driven off to such far-flung places as Swanage and Corfe Castle – what excitement!

I was astonished when the planners allowed the Institute to be pulled down and then the site was built on (now Moule Terrace). That building

Reverend Henry Moule. (Courtesy of Dorset County Museum.)

Moule's earth closet, improved version circa 1875. (Source: By User Musphot on Wikimedia Commons.) What a pity my aunt in Piddlehinton had not heard of this, much preferred to a bucket and newspaper.

should have been allowed to stand, perhaps as a museum of Fordington, commemorating the Reverend Moule, vicar of Fordington between 1829 and 1880, who did so much to improve the life of his parishioners, especially during the time of cholera. He is famous for inventing the earth closet.

The Boys' School in Colliton Street

David Forrester, a cheeky school boy aged 7 or 8.

At the age of 7 the boys transferred to St Peter's Institute, the boys' school in Colliton Street, and the girls went to Maud Road School. The school badge was red on black with two crossed keys, the latter being a symbol for St Peter. Many of us wore shoes or boots that were the wrong size and much of the clothing never fitted, as hand-me-downs were the order of the day.

Haircuts were what we called basin cuts; a pudding basin was put on your head and the hair trimmed round, giving quite a funny look. Lots of boys were to be seen with brown patches caused by the liberal use of iodine on various cuts or scratches. Also sores on the body were much in evidence, often coated in what they called Gentian Violet, causing large purple-coloured patches on the skin. I think if you met one of these boys today you would give him a wide berth!

My memories of this school, where I stayed until the age of 11, are mixed. The school was based in a main block at the top of Colliton Street, with two additional classrooms in Grey School Passage, and two more at the bottom of the road in what was originally St Peter's Institute.

You entered the main school building through gates into the playground. On the left was the cookhouse where frequently you could smell cabbage,

The Boys Brigade and School Cadet Corps outside the old school in Colliton Street, 1915. (Courtesy of Les Philips.)

The old Dorchester Youth Centre with the school behind, long since gone and replaced by flats. (Courtesy of Les Philips.)

St Peter's Institute at the bottom of Colliton Street; we walked up and down the road according to lessons. The building is now used for storage by the Dorset County Museum.

already boiling at 8.30 am ready for lunch. School dinners served here were some of the worst food I was ever forced to eat. I especially hated sago and tapioca with a spoonful of jam in the middle. My first teacher, Miss Dominie, took an instant dislike to me and punished me for any misdemeanor, often blaming me for what others had done. The headmaster, Mr Truella, never missed a chance to say how much better my brother had been than me: 'If only you were like your brother!' I can still hear

Old school classrooms in Grey School Passage.

this ringing in my ears. My brother had been at the school a full 7 years before me. Could Mr Truella never forget?

As a church school, religious teaching played a large part in the curriculum. Each Friday morning we were marched in pairs down Grey School Passage to attend assembly in Holy Trinity Church. I particularly enjoyed this, especially the hymn singing; I suppose I also enjoyed the fact that we were missing lessons.

The school had no playing field so we exercised in the playground. Sometimes we played Shinty; this was a very rough game, played in the yard opposite the school gates, now the District Council car park. The game was played with a stick very much like a walking stick and a ball. I suppose it was a bit like hockey. The two things I remember are that the ball wasn't allowed to go above shoulder height and that you always ended up with bruised and painful shins. Perhaps that's why it was called Shinty? On special days we were bussed or walked to Weymouth Avenue to play cricket or run races on the Dorchester sports ground. This always excited us as the procedure took the whole afternoon and was preferable to almost anything else. One of the things we also much enjoyed was country dancing, surprising for an all-boys school. We learned quite a few different dances and one summer went to a competition of sorts at Wareham.

The forge in Colliton Street, 1959. (Courtesy of Dorset County Museum.)

Opposite St Peter's Institute was the forge of Mr Tucker, the blacksmith. It was here that I first met Les Philips, a

Mr Tucker and Les Philips hard at work in the forge. There was no shortage of horses requiring shoeing in those days. (Courtesy of Les Philips.)

raw young apprentice, destined to become Mayor of Dorchester on no less than four occasions. Owners would bring their horses to the blacksmith's shop and leave them in the stalls at the back, much as you would leave a car for service today. The old shoes would be removed from the hoof and new ones modelled on the anvil. While still hot these shoes would be applied to the hoof with a hiss and a puff of smoke, the smell of burning horn not one you would forget for the rest of your life.

Virgin, the bakers. The sign in the window reads 'Hovis Bread, as supplied to H.M. the King'. The premises are now Wedding Time (a somewhat ironic following to the old name). (Courtesy of Dorset County Museum.)

Attending the Boys' School meant we had to walk on our own from home in Fordington through the town and up Grey School Passage: this always seemed to us a great adventure. On the way we would pass Virgin, 'Pastry Cook and Confectioner', selling lovely buns and cream cakes. Down the side was the bake house where we could buy a bag of stale cakes for a penny. These cakes were then sold on for a farthing each or swapped for other goods or favours when we reached school.

Being very close by, we had wonderful nature walks down to the river and along to Blue Bridge. We carried jam jars and returned with all sorts of catches, which were added to the nature corner at the front of the classroom. Each class was always proud of its nature table with sticky buds, flowers and things such as frog spawn and tadpoles at various times of the year. We were taught to appreciate our surroundings, love nature and treat it with care.

In the early 1950s, the path to Blue Bridge had clear, clean water running on both sides. John's pond once contained crystal-clear water fed by the

Blue Bridge was as far as we went on our nature trips from school. We clutched our jam jars as if they were gold dust, returning with prized minnows, sticklebacks and lampreys.

John's Pond, an idyllic spot next to Hangman's Cottage.

stream, which used to run down the right-hand side of the path leading to Blue Bridge; this is now filled in and water enters the pond under the lock gate from the main river on the other side. At one end of John's Pond there was sand on which parents would take their children to play, it was like a trip to the beach.

On the way home from school we again passed through the town, usually running down the left-hand side of the road. On our way we would jump up and touch the bars of the awnings hanging outside many of the shops. One particular day one lad swung on the bar outside Jackmans Clothiers, bringing the awning crashing down. The next day the head asked the culprit to own up. Needless to say no one did, but after that we walked down the other side of the street for quite some time.

Next door to the Corn Exchange, Jackmans, the gentleman's outfitters for so many years. All school clothes and uniform came from here. The name is still evident today in the floor of the old shop entrance way.

Carey Camp

One of the most exciting things we did in our last year at the Boys' School was to visit Carey Camp at Wareham for four nights. We caught the bus to Carey and suddenly we were cast into a whole new world.

In those days facilities were very poor. The tents were already erected and we were allocated one, six pupils to each tent. Here we placed our 'bed' on the ground sheet; this was made up of a couple of blankets folded over and pinned with blanket pins to make a sort of sleeping bag. We were then taken on a tour of the facilities, if you could call them that. Washing consisted of one long trough with a row of cold taps fixed above, and washing in the morning was swift, the water being so cold that basically it was a waste of time. For the urinals you simply stood above a small trench. The toilet was a much deeper trench with a long wooden seat fixed above it with holes at intervals; between each hole hung a bit of tarpaulin, as if this gave you any privacy. This whole lot was in an open-ended tin shack. Believe me, you didn't go there any more often than was absolutely necessary.

The first night we were put to bed and after a short while told it was lights out. A few of us had torches so of course we chattered and were told to stop, which we didn't as basically we were overexcited. So we were taken outside and caned by Mr Woodward, whose favourite thing in life was to thrash boys. He never missed a chance. At this time we were also reminded that we

Carey Camp in the 1950s. (Courtesy of Carey Camp, Sally Wales, Dorset County Council.)

must not get up before 6.45 am. None of us had a watch, so this instruction was a waste of time. In the morning we awoke to the sound of voices, quickly dressed, splashed our faces with water and went to swing on a rope hanging from a tree. As we were all swinging happily, our swings accompanied by the obligatory Tarzan cries, Mr Woodward arrived on the scene accompanied by his trusty cane. The time, we were informed, was 5.15 am. Having been duly punished, we returned to our tent to scrabble under our blankets, too scared to talk, awaiting our 6.45 am call.

Having learned the rules the hard way, we had a wonderful time at Carey. Much of our time was spent learning about the countryside and wildlife; we also learned a lot about ourselves and about one another. One afternoon a paper chase kept us very much amused. We loved the singing, fun and games around the camp fire each evening. On the last night we had a midnight feast in our tent with a tuck parcel my mum had sent me from the shop. We shared the biscuits, etc. in total silence of course, not even daring to mumble or whisper. Surprisingly for 10-year-olds who had never been away alone, we nearly all stuck it out and enjoyed it, despite the hard conditions. Only one boy left due to home sickness.

In 2002 as Chair of Governors of Cerne Abbas First School I visited our children at Carey Camp with the headmistress Jean Riley. What a change, what luxury! A smart toilet block, hot water, showers; obviously the modern child could never understand how tough we had it.

Dorchester Secondary Modern School

Following failure of the 11+ Exam, much to the disgust of my father, I moved to the Modern School in Coburg Road. It was where I wanted to go anyway; for a start, Thomas Hardye School boys went to school on Saturday mornings and that was definitely out of the question (Saturdays were for play!). Having attended small schools up to this date, joining a school with 750 pupils was quite a shock.

In the beginning we went by bus from Fordington Green, then after a couple of years we were allowed to ride our bikes. For the first few days we all rushed to sit upstairs on the bus; however, I soon changed to sitting downstairs, in safety with Miss Vincent, out of the way of the bullies. Miss Vincent was actually Deputy Head, filling in as Head while we waited for a new Head, and things were great. After Christmas the new Head arrived –

Mr Harry Dawe, soon to be 'Jackdaw' to us. He was not like Miss Vincent and he and I didn't get off to a good start.

It would have been the beginning of January 1954 when we were having snow. At his second assembly the message he gave us in the strongest possible terms was no snowballing in the quadrangle. The next morning, with a new cover of snow, this message was totally forgotten as total war broke out. Throughout my school days I counted myself as unlucky. Having just been hit with a large snowball, I fired off a retaliatory shot. At that moment Jackdaw came around the corner from the car park, to be greeted by a snowball which smashed against the wall next to him. 'What's your name, boy?' (he never needed to ask that question again). 'Forrester, Sir,' I replied. 'Forrester, wait outside my office, I will deal with you later.' So the long wait, which presumably was part of the punishment, then the standard punishment of 'six of the best' – life under the rule of Jackdaw had begun.

Later I was much amused when having done very well in my chosen career as Purchasing and Logistics Manager for a large American company I was able to retire at the age of 56 and move back to Dorchester. As a Rotarian I joined the Rotary Club of Dorchester. There on the Board listing the Presidents was the name H. Dawe. In the year 2005 when I became President, my name was duly added. I'm not sure, but I think I felt old Jackdaw turn in his grave. No one reading this book can realise what satisfaction that gave me.

The Modern School was great for boys like me. Apart from normal lessons we had plots of ground on which we could grow our own crops, under supervision. There were pigs, chickens, hives of bees and a greenhouse. We also had an afternoon of metalwork and one of woodwork on alternate weeks. All of this I believe gave

Rotarian H.J. Dawe, President in 1965, recorded on the board hanging in the King's Arms Hotel. Never in a million years would he have guessed that he would be followed in 2005 by D.J. Forrester, that horrible boy he caned so often and once said, 'I dread to think what will become of you!'

29

us invaluable experience that we could and indeed did use long into the future. Mr Bonfield, the woodwork teacher, had a large poster at the front of the class which read 'Measure twice, cut once'; this is something I have tried to do ever since then. It is good guidance if you are working with materials, and also in daily life when transferred to 'Think twice, act once' – certainly good advice.

For some weeks, instead of woodwork or metalwork we helped build a school swimming pool at the top of the playing field, very rewarding work. It was quite sad that the older boys, who actually carried out most of the work, had left school by the time the pool was opened and therefore received no benefit for their hard labour. When the pool was finished we all went for our first swim. This exciting morning soon turned sour when some of us knelt down to feel the temperature of the water with our hands. As punishment for this we were caned by the games master on the rear, not with a cane but with a cricket stump; believe me, the bruises were a sight to be seen. Usually when I was punished at school I kept it from my father, as if he found out he would clip my ear and say I must have deserved it. However, on this occasion I could not sit down at all, the bruising was so severe. The day being a Friday, the next morning my father, for the first time ever, thought that the punishment did not fit the crime and I was taken to Jackdaw's house in Fordington. Mr Dawe was not at home but his wife invited us in. My father explained why we were there and then made me drop my trousers and pants; I was 14 years old and I don't have to tell you how embarrassing this was. I later heard father tell my mother that Mrs Dawe nearly fainted when she saw the damage that six blows of a cricket stump can do. On Monday morning I was summoned to the Head's office, not for punishment for once but for the games master to apologise.

A toast rack, cigarette box and table made at school. The metalwork items my mother had silver-plated and they won me a certificate at the Dorset Arts and Crafts Show in Wareham

Sometimes it was difficult to understand the punishment that was handed out. But a particular naughty incident of mine comes to mind. One of our great things was to have pet slow worms. I had a little favourite called Silver, about 4 inches long and very thin. I sometimes carried Silver to school in my pocket and one of my tricks was to slip him into my mouth. One day the girl at the desk in front of me looked around and I opened the corner of my mouth and Silver poked his nose out. The young lady let out a piercing scream. This caused mayhem. By the time the teacher asked me about the incident, Silver was safely back in my pocket. Of course he was soon discovered, after I was called to the front of the class and had to empty my pockets. I was made to take Silver down by the side of our allotment plots and let him go, and that was the last time he was seen. On my return the usual punishment was dished out. Strangely enough a few days later when the young lady put on her coat to go home, she found a frog in her pocket; they never did catch the culprit.

Some of the lessons I did enjoy were chemistry and biology. So I was quite happy when asked to call at the Slaughter House at the bottom of Fordington Hill and collect some bullock's eyes which we were to dissect. Little did I know what an awful job this was to be. As it turned out, the eyes had been roughly cut out and were surrounded by fat, blood and gristle. The sack I was given containing the eyes was covered in blood which was dripping everywhere and very heavy, and in retrospect I suppose I should have refused to take it. However, I was young and determined to carry out the task. So I hung the sack in the frame of my bike and pushed the bike to school, leaving a trail behind me and gaining interest from several cats and dogs on the way. On reaching school, I was very tired, had blood on my trousers and didn't know what to do. The science lab was on the second floor and I knew to get there would leave a bloody trail. So I went to the lab to explain. I was met with the comment 'Forrester, you're late'. 'I think you'd better come and look, sir,' I said. The teacher joined me in the walk back to the bike shed. When he undid the sack and looked in he exclaimed, 'Good God, Forrester. I'm sorry, I didn't expect this!' For a few days afterwards people teased me with 'Eye-eye, Forrester'.

I can't finish without mention of the Magpies, Dorchester's football team, which was followed by all us boys. One Wednesday afternoon Dorchester was playing Weymouth in a cup replay. That morning at assembly the strict warning was given not to think we could get away with going to the match, as the register would be checked. So we duly went to the first lesson and to registration, then as we moved on to the next lesson we slipped off down

The Magpies, with Dorchester Town legend Dennis 'Dinky' Curtis (second left front row). (Courtesy of Mrs Helen Curtis.)

The Magpies off to Bayeux for a twinning football match. Notice the old Dorset County Stores in the background. (Courtesy of Mrs Helen Curtis.)

the road. There was quite a crowd so we sat up on top of the corrugated iron fence, which was uncomfortable but gave us a good view. However, we were interrupted by a loud cry of 'You boys, I know who you are. Be outside the Head's office first thing in the morning!' That spoilt our day. The next morning we lined up for the usual long wait to receive the cane. We were then told the bad news; we were all banned from going to the end-of-term Christmas party. That really hit us.

The end of term came with the Carol Service in the United Church, South Street – I believe Mr Dawe was a lay preacher at the time – to be followed in the evening by the party. At the service, as I had done several times before, I sang in the choir, also singing a solo, the first verse of *Once in Royal David's City*. As we filed out at the end of the service I was approached by Jackdaw who said, 'Forrester, you sang beautifully. I think you have redeemed yourself, you may go to the party tonight'. I rushed home to tell mum I was going to the party, only to be asked why I hadn't mentioned it before. Of course I had

Mr Griffin, the choir master, with the choir carol singing at the Cenotaph (I am in school cap glancing up at my friend's sister Linda Colbourne).

not said anything about being banned as this would have just brought more punishment from my father. The party was much enjoyed, but unfortunately the next day I received another sort of punishment from my friends, who felt I should have refused unless they could also go.

So the four years at the Modern School passed quickly and at the age of 15 in 1958 my school days were over. I left school and worked on a farm in West Stafford, then went to Kingston Maurward College, but realised I didn't want to spend the rest of my life feeding and clearing up after animals. I furthered my education at evening classes, college and through correspondence classes. How many times I wished I had worked harder at school. My school reports all said the same –'Could do better!'

Note: I have kept the school days together to make them easy to follow, and therefore the rest of these pages are not in strict chronological order.

Times they are a-changing

In the late 1940s High West and High East Streets were the main shopping streets, boasting no less than five general grocery shops, bakers, butchers and nine pubs. People walking in from villages like Bockhampton could get all their shopping before they reached the town clock on the Corn

Looking down High East Street, 1959. (Courtesy of Les Philips.)

Exchange. They didn't have to carry the goods home, as in those days they were delivered by a boy on a bike with a basket on the front. South Street was where the great and the good of Dorchester had lived in large houses in past years, but gradually this street began filling up with shops.

Meat and game used to hang outside Hodder's, the butchers (now Masala's Indian restaurant). Here you waited to be served, clasping coupons from the ration book and a note from mum. Mr Hodder or Mr Dunford

Prize-winning Christmas turkeys in the window of Hodder's in High East Street in the 1950s. (Courtesy of Dorset County Museum.)

would cut and chop the required meat, then wrap it, often with a couple of sausages or a lump of lard. The little extra was always well received on returning home: 'Mr Hodder's a real Christian' or 'That lovely man!' often was said when my mother unwrapped the parcel.

At the bottom of the High Street by the White Hart public house there was a ford to play in, but this disappeared with the building of the new bridge in 1954, a cause of great excitement. For a start they worked not only during the day, but also at night, using floodlights. Even more exciting, the hatches were closed and the river was redirected, leaving the riverbed mainly dry and muddy with some large puddles. Each of us lads had a stick with a fork

In 1954 the river was redirected and a bridge by the White Hart was built. The river now ran under the bridge and behind Lott & Walne to form the Mill Stream.

The Mill Stream behind Lott & Walne. Beyond this point police were only allowed to walk in pairs.

on the end, and we walked along the riverbed turning over stones in pools and spearing eels; we also came upon the odd sorry trout that had become trapped there.

Outside the back of the White Hart over the River Frome some toilets were built. We used to play around, running in and knocking on the doors. One day my friends rolled a banger under an 'engaged' door. The next day they returned to find the same toilet apparently still engaged; this had us really worried. Bending down to look under the door, it opened and,

Toilets over the river. I have never seen any like them before or since.

looking up into the face of the emerging man, they cried, 'We thought you was dead!' Sometime in the late 1960s these toilets were demolished, but you can still see where they stood over the river.

Market days

During the holidays, Dorchester, being a market town, was a great attraction for us. The Wednesday market was held in Weymouth Avenue, as it is now, though it was a cattle market then. Milking cows, calves and pigs were all sold in the auction ring, which is now used to market farm-produced meat, sausages and eggs. The cows were not always moved to the buyer's farm until the next day, so they were milked where they stood by men willing to undertake this for some free milk. In the undercover part of the market were cages containing live hens, cockerels, rabbits, etc. I once put my finger through the wire in the ferret cage to try to stroke one, but a ferret sank its teeth into my finger right down to the bone and wouldn't let go. All the dead chicken, rabbits and so on were hung over rails in another part of the covered area. Also undercover were the eggs (duck, chicken and goose).

The local carrier had a big part to play on market day transporting people and produce. Quite often eggs, chickens and ducks, both alive and killed and plucked, were collected from different cottages by a carrier on his way to town. These were then sold and on the way back home the cash for the produce would be dropped off; a great deal of trust was involved in an operation like that. Another market was held on Saturdays in Charles Street in the area that is now a car park; this consisted more of beef animals, pigs and the odd sheep to clear.

Sheep fairs were held as separate occasions, either at Poundbury or on Fair Field where the market car park is now in Weymouth Avenue. Some days before, a great number of pens would be made using hurdles. Sheep would be driven along the roads from as far away as Blandford, Sherborne and Bridport. They would be rested in fields overnight around Dorchester and in the morning driven into town for the fair. Just imagine trying to do this today.

Market days were always eventful when people from the surrounding villages came to town for the day. For many it was the only outing of the week, and with holidays being out of the question, market days were looked forward to. The pubs were especially busy on these days, and farmers struck many a deal in them, probably somewhat affected by the drink.

The sheep fair in Dorchester. (Courtesy of Dorset County Museum.)

Gypsies in town

Gypsies were regularly to be seen in the community, selling small posies of flowers or knocking on doors to sell pegs. One family, the Benhams, lived in caravans on a plot at the corner of Piddle Lane and Slyer's Lane. They were a good lot and never caused any trouble. One of them, Marky (Ben), was a dwarf about 3 ft tall, well known by everyone. He always wore a tie but never learned to put it on himself but carried it to town and would ask the first person he met to tie it for him. This would always be followed by, 'Have you got a light?' If the answer was yes, the next question was 'Have you got a fag?' People always knew what was coming but nobody really minded; of course we all smoked in those days.

Marky was the only gypsy that landlord Harry Grigg allowed into the White Hart pub and he earned his beer with his party trick which was to pick up pennies. Twelve of these large coins were placed in a stack on the floor. Marky would then stand on his hands, lower his head down and pick up all twelve pennies in his mouth; if he left one, he didn't get to keep any, but he never failed.

On occasions there would be a gypsy funeral in the town; this always meant trouble. They would be in town for several days and it would all start okay, men would be seen with huge wads of cash, buying and selling horses. The deal done, they would spit on their hand and slap the other man's hand.

Lots of pubs banned them, but they always managed to end up drunk and fighting would break out, with more and more men joining in. These fights were in fact not much different from some of the scenes played out in the 'Wild West' films of the time.

Once there was a Gypsy Queen's funeral that brought gypsies from everywhere; they packed the town. The police had a busy time trying to sort out fights in one area or another. As children we were most amazed when we saw blood all over the pavement. The final part of the funeral was to burn the Queen's caravan down at the water meadows, something that caused quite a stir. Was the Queen's body still in the caravan?

Weekend entertainment

At a very young age we boys experienced freedom that no modern child will see today and we made our own entertainment for much of the time. We may not have travelled in the way today's children do, but of Dorchester and the surrounding area we knew every nook and cranny.

The weekend was something we always looked forward to, especially Saturday mornings, as it was our chance to go to the cinema. At home, our only entertainment was the radio. How much I enjoyed sitting with my father on a winter evening in front of the fire with the lights out. In the flickering light there was this wonderful atmosphere, and then the echoing words 'Journey into Space' would signal the beginning of my favourite programme. Other favourites were Dick Barton Special Agent and PC49. However, the cinema, that really was something special. We all joined the children's club at the Palace Cinema and we wore our C Club badge with pride. The Palace was in Durngate Street opposite what is now the Dinosaur Museum. A block of flats now stands on the site, the only reference to the cinema being the name, Palace Court. I suspect few of the present residents realise the significance of the name.

We all arrived on Saturday morning early, clasping our 3d entrance fees. The films were black-and-white, and some involving chase scenes were silent. Many were westerns with Roy Rogers, Gabby Hayes, Tom Mix, Buffalo Bill and of course the Lone Ranger and Tonto. A comedy, 'The Bowery Boys', was another favourite, also Laurel and Hardy. How we loved these films, which were produced for children's Cinema Clubs all over the country. To us at a young age this was serious stuff, and shouts such as 'Look out – behind you!' were often to be heard when Roy Rogers was in trouble. Several of the films were in the form of serials and this meant you had to go the following Saturday. Many children too ill to go to school Thursday or Friday made miraculous recoveries on Saturday just in time for the cinema.

Simple things used to please us; on a Saturday afternoon we would go to South Street and one of our tricks was to stand outside the old Woolworths store (now Poundland) staring at the roof of Barclays Bank opposite. After a while other people would start to look up. We would then walk off to the bottom of the street and back. On our return we would see how many people were still looking up. Once you got it going, it was amazing how many people you could get to look at absolutely nothing. I'm sure it would still work today.

Another cause of excitement was when the Dorset Regiment came into town. The Regiment was given the Freedom of Dorchester which meant they could march through town supported by crowds of onlookers. Some of the veterans would come behind, one or two in wheelchairs. I remember seeing one of the last soldiers alive who had fought in the Crimean War, which ended in 1856.

The Dorset Regiment marching down Dorchester High Street. (Courtesy of Les Philips.

St George's Church

From the age of seven I joined St George's Church choir, and singing and the church were a great part of my life until I was 16. Returning to Dorset 40 years later, I discovered that the choir mistress Evelyn Kingman was still there – what devotion to duty. I became a soloist and now in my retirement I still sing in the Casterbridge Male Voice Choir.

All of us choir boys went to practice on Tuesday (boys only) and Friday (full choir). We always arrived early and played in the churchyard, collecting slow worms from around the gravestones. On Friday the whole choir practised and after an hour the boys were allowed to go and the adults rehearsed on their own. Let loose on dark evenings we had great fun, such as hanging the choirmaster's bike in the holly tree. In winter we all had torches and would split up into two groups. One group would hunt the other down and if you were caught in the beam of the torch, you were pronounced dead and out of the game. On occasions we would get into the back of the tower, having unlocked the door earlier, and would plunge the church into darkness by

Being in the choir holds special memories for me, particularly the times before and after choir practice. Rev. Jessop is front right, with Mr Barber, the choir master, and Evelyn Kingman (third row, centre) who gave over 60 years' service to the church.

pulling the main switch. Someone from the choir would then have to find their way from the chapel at the front to the tower at the back to pull the switch and put the lights back on.

The vicar at that time was the Rev. Gilbert Jessop; he was a great cricketer who played for Dorchester and the county. St George's also had a good team and we could practise in the nets, which were situated where the new vicarage now stands. Gilbert's father was an even more famous cricketer known as 'the Croucher' who played many games for England. When Gilbert moved into the vicarage his father was quite elderly, although still sprightly, and he loved to join in playing conkers or marbles with us lads. The sad thing is we didn't realise how famous the old chap was until he died. Then it was in all the papers and for some time after his death people would come from all over the country to view his grave.

'The Croucher' G.L. Jessop, 1874–1955. (Photo by E. Hawkins from Wikipedia Commons). His grave is in Fordington churchyard.

These were the years when the church played a much larger part in our lives than it ever does for children in this day and age. I was a server for communion, and at that time we had communion at 7, 8 and 9 am, a morning service at 11 am, bible study at 2.30 pm and evensong at 6 pm. It is amazing to think that all these were well attended, and many people would go to church on three occasions on a Sunday. We boys kept up a good attendance record. I think we were paid a penny (1d) a service and sometimes a shilling for weddings. There was also an award for the boy with the best overall attendance; he won the right to wear the attendance badge on a ribbon around his neck. On St George's Day and Ascension Day at 7 am we all climbed the tower to sing hymns. This was followed by a cooked breakfast served in the Moule Institute by the ladies of the church.

Gilbert Jessop was a great friend to us boys. It was clear that his first love in life was cricket; he just happened to be also a priest. Gilbert would spend hours in the nets teaching us the rudiments of cricket. He quite often struggled to get up for the 7 o'clock service. I would have to knock at his door and throw stones at his window. One day my efforts to wake him caused a badly cracked window in the vicarage. This was the one time in my childhood that I broke a window and was not severely chastised.

On another occasion we had no bread for the 7 o'clock communion, only some stale bread with mould on left over from the midweek communion. I was instructed to slice off the mould and cut it into squares (rice paper wafers were not yet invented). At least no one seemed to notice. I looked on, hardly able to hide my smile, as the congregation received their communion that morning.

Many times I have thrown stones at the windows of Fordington Vicarage to wake Gilbert for the 7 am service. Now I note the building has been turned into flats and fitted with double glazing.

The wall at the side of the church overlooked Daubenys Farm, now a car park in front of some flats built in the old farmyard (there is no evidence of the farm today). The cows were brought up for milking from the meadows in London Road beyond Grey's Bridge. They were walked to the farm by way of Kings Road to Fordington Cross and up the hill. If you were really lucky Maurice Daubeny would allow you to ride on the back of the carthorse to collect the cows. Some years later Mr Daubeny acquired a milking bale, a mobile shelter with a vacuum pump attached, which could be moved from field to field with a tractor. From then on the twice-daily walk up the hill to be milked stopped and things were never quite the same in Fordington.

No. 20 High Street Fordington, formerly Rolls Dairy. From here Mr Rolls and his two sons left while we were all tucked up in bed, to deliver milk in bottles to our doorstep.

Fordington Hill from the Cross as it was when we brought the cows up from the meadows to be milked at the farm next to the church. (Courtesy of T. Hearing.)

Mr Daubeny's cows in the water meadows. (Copyright Mill Street Housing Society.)

Growing up in Fordington

Climbing, riding, running free.
Going fishing? Wait for me.
Scrumping apples? Take your pick,
There's 'Old Bony', scatter quick.

Haunted houses. Don't you dare!
Slow worms here and lizards there.
Out of bounds, nowhere at all.
Church on Sunday, choir boys all.

Little angels in a row
Which one let that big frog go?
Bows and arrows, you should die.
See that buzzard in the sky?

Squirrel's dray and badger's set,
Are the chestnuts ready yet?
Bridging rivers, damming streams.
Home wet footed to sweet dreams.

Of course the real joy in those times was the freedom we had. We were free to roam the countryside, the woods, fields and rivers, for several miles around Dorchester, and we knew them all. Once we were older and had our bikes we travelled even further, though the bikes themselves usually left something to be desired. For a boy in Fordington in 1950 a new bike was something you only dreamed about. Most of us had pass-me-downs or multicoloured cycles made from several parts picked up from the scrap yard at the bottom of Durngate Street (now garages). This yard was also the place where we took our rabbit skins when mother had a rabbit given to her. Rabbit stew meant something special to us, only because we received a few pence for the skin. In those days this was a king's ransom to us.

Also from this scrap yard came the glass battery-cases (accumulators) about 9 inches square by 15 inches high. These cases were soaked and scrubbed until they were sparkling clean, for originally they had contained acid. They were then filled with water and used to keep tadpoles, minnows, sticklebacks or goldfish. We even had one at school on the nature table. Sticklebacks were particularly interesting, as unlike other fish, they built a small oval nest, and discovering one of these was wonderful.

Our constant trips to the countryside gave us a great understanding of animals. I am sorry to say, we all had large collections of birds' eggs. At that time we didn't realise the harm we were doing. We also had all sorts of different pets: rabbits (sadly often eaten), newts, lizards, slow worms, hedgehogs, tadpoles and of course frogs. We quite often picked up wounded animals and then tried to nurse them back to health, mostly hidden away from our parents who became quite fed up with our adopted friends.

One such friend was Jack the Jackdaw. He lived with me for a couple of years, and he went everywhere sitting on my shoulder. Jack never entered the house; my mother hated it and father put up with it. Mr Woodward, our teacher at the time, would have happily killed it. The class, needless to say, thought it was good fun. Jack would accompany me to school sitting on my shoulder or flapping from one spot to another. When we reached school Jack would spend the time perched on the windowsill looking in at the class. The windows had to remain closed, following his second visit to the classroom. One sad day, Jack, who must have fancied a young Jill, flew off and was never seen again.

During my early years at 35 High Street, my grandparents lived with us. They also had lost their house during the war. For some of this time grandfather worked at Rodgers Gardens on London Road next to the river; the area was later used as a caravan site and now has flats built on it (Swanbridge Court). However, at this time the land was covered in gardens and some fine heated greenhouses stood here for many years. Grandfather worked in these gardens with our neighbour Charlie Brake. The plot of ground, like the allotments further along the river path opposite Frome Terrace, was extremely fertile and grew wonderful crops. The only drawback was that it was prone to flooding. Sometimes in the winter the ground was under water for several days. One of the problems with this was that the boiler for heating the greenhouses was set in a pit 7 or 8 ft below ground level (all boiler houses seemed to be like that). When the water rose the boiler was soon flooded and when it receded the pit had to be bailed out. Together with Charlie's lad Tony, a great friend,

I used to be tasked with this, and at the time this wet and mucky job seemed quite exciting. When the water was gone the boiler had to be dried and relit, and this often proved to be a difficult job.

My grandfather also did other jobs in the countryside around Dorchester. He often came home with a rabbit, hare, pheasant, woodcock, or perhaps some eels from the trap. We never asked where they came from! When I look back, from a food point of view, we lived very well, for grandfather also had an allotment, as did a great many people at that time. When still quite small I remember him bringing home a bundle tied in a knot and placing it on the kitchen floor. When left alone I investigated the bundle and found that it moved. Dragging

Aerial view showing the wonderfully productive Rodgers Gardens, where vegetables and flowers were grown to supply Rodgers shops in High West Street and South Street and other wholesalers. (Courtesy of Dorset County Museum.)

it under the kitchen table I managed to undo the knot, releasing a dozen eels which wriggled all over the floor, leaving a horrible slimy trail wherever they went.

One of the things that stand out in my memory is the way that the whole family worked together when there was a job to be done. When the shallots were ready we would all sit around an old tin bath and tackle them, taking off the skins and throwing the bulbs into the salt water brine to soak overnight prior to pickling and bottling. The next day a huge amount of spiced vinegar had to be made up. This mixture was placed in a huge boiler on top of the stove, and the smell was incredible. In season, runner beans would be sliced by us all in huge quantities and salted down in empty sweet jars from the shop (no freezers then). When rinsed and cooked these beans were an awful greeny-yellow colour and didn't taste much better than they looked. Also huge amounts of blackcurrants and gooseberries would be brought home in boxes and we would sit topping and tailing them ready for bottling in Kilner jars.

When it came to the time to make Christmas cakes and puddings, all the raisins, sultanas and currants had to be picked over, the stones taken out and small stems removed. The prepared fruit then had to be washed and laid out on an assortment of trays to dry. How much easier things are today. However, times spent doing these jobs were very enjoyable as three generations sat around and talked. In today's society, the opportunity for these conversations seems less frequent.

Behind our home ran Holloway Road which led to the Mill Street area of Dorchester. This area was rather a slum and the river that ran through it was filled with rubbish – old prams, bikes, tin baths and other assorted things. Many of the houses were in a bad state of repair, and the gardens were filled with trash. At the end of each garden stood a small upright shed with a badly fitting door; this was the toilet, which in winter must have been cold. For Fordington lads the quickest route to Grey's Bridge and thus onwards to Pigeon Copse, a small wood across the fields from Slyer's Lane, or to Bockhampton was through Mill Street. We would head up Holloway Road, down the steps and over a small river bridge (still there) into Mill Street, cutting through between the houses. This route always kept us on our toes, as there was often no love lost between us and the children of Mill Street. At this time the police were only allowed to go beyond the White Hart into Fordington in pairs as the area was well known for trouble.

(Copyright Mill Street Housing Society.)

(Copyright Mill Street Housing Society.)

Much of the danger as we ran through there was of course imagined. Many of the people were no different from us, but they were living in an area that left much to be desired. Even in 1950 many were living in poverty and some of the children were indeed our schoolmates. My mother owning a shop meant we didn't have a lot of money but we always had full stomachs. This could not be said for those in Mill Street, or indeed some other areas of Dorchester. When, for instance, I went to school with an apple, there were always plenty who would say, 'Give us your core'. Can you imagine that now?

In Mill Street many of the families were large, and one had fifteen children. I was in the class with the twins from that family. Though some of the older children had grown up and left home before the last ones were born, just imagine living in the houses as they did with that number of children and very little money. Throughout my life, when my own children have complained about this or that, I have looked back at those times and thought, if only you knew the meaning of the words 'cold' or 'hungry'. I can remember undressing under the bedclothes and getting up in the morning to write my name on the ice on the inside of my bedroom window.

We often ate mackerel, at that time both plentiful and cheap. Early on summer mornings or evenings, the call of 'Mackerel, mackerel, fresh Weymouth mackerel' would alert you to the fact that these fish were for sale. One man traded from the back of an old Ford van, the other from a box carefully balanced on top of a basket at the front of his bike. The day came when my mother would not buy from the bike man. He had been seen, early one morning down by the White Hart, dipping his box of fish in the river to ensure they looked shiny and fresh. Having purchased the fish they were either fried or soused in vinegar and eaten cold. As a boy I loved mackerel; however, if I ate too much it would bring me out in a rash. In later years I was happy to discover several other people who had had the same problem.

Another regular visitor to Fordington was the rag and bone man. There was never any doubt about when he had arrived with his cart, drawn by a friendly old horse; his cry of 'Any old rags, bottles or bones?' could be heard several streets away. When we were at St George's Infants School, it was quite upsetting to hear this cry, as you knew you had missed a chance of earning a penny or two by getting something from mother to give to him.

One of the things we made in those days to amuse ourselves was a sort of telephone. All we needed were two cocoa tins and a long piece of thin string. A hole was made in the bottom of each tin and one end of the string was pushed through each tin and tied in a knot. When pulled tight and one person said something into the tin, the person the other end could hear them if they put the tin to their ear. I and Tony who lived next door had one of these rigged up. It would hang loosely through each of our bedroom windows. If we wanted to speak we would jerk the line gently to alert the person the other end, who would then pull the string tight and a conversation could start.

Fishing

Fishing was, with all us lads, a major part of our entertainment. All the rivers around Dorchester were teaming with trout at the time. We became experts at dodging the water bailiff, who was of course paid to ensure we caught as few trout as possible, though he had very little success. Many of the houses around the Frome were near to the river and we all fished with hand lines, using bread as bait (being a staple food, cheap and soon going stale, much bread ended up in the river). While we fished, a lookout was kept all the time for the bailiff who had a pair of binoculars; sometimes we could see them in the hedge glinting in the sunlight. If we were not fishing but just mooching around and saw him, we would pretend to be fishing and wait for him to sneak up on us. He would shout, 'Got you this time, you ruffians!' We would reply, 'What, us? Fishing?' Mind you, we did have some close shaves. On one occasion we didn't see him until the last moment and had to quickly hide our lines before he was upon us; not only that but he stood with his feet only inches away from a particularly large trout hidden in the long grass. Eventually satisfied he moved off and we collapsed in an exhausted heap.

Another time we came upon a friend near the swimming baths, the other side of Grey's Bridge. He had just caught a pike about 2 ft long and didn't want it, so I decided to take it home, having heard they were good to eat. I clonked it on the head and stuffed it down my shirt with its head in the top

Many a good trout was caught in the waters beneath Grey's Bridge.

Now barely recognisable, the hatches have gone and the concrete sides of the old river baths are overgrown.

of my trousers. Half way home the fish began to wriggle, but that wasn't the worst bit; it slipped further down to my crotch and started to open and close its mouth. Now I had seen its row of sharp teeth and could sense danger. I had to grab it as best I could and run faster and faster, breaking out in a right sweat. I didn't do that again!

When we were older one bailiff, Mr Bowditch, an ex-policeman, became quite friendly with us and by then we were buying fishing licences and had realised that he was quite happy for us to catch pike as they were eating the trout. However, he still didn't know what we were really up to. He had a number of wicker work traps that he set at various points in the river. Of course we knew where the traps were and, all being early risers, would check them before he arrived in the morning, on occasions adjusting the contents of the trap according to our whim. We would ask 'Much in the traps today?' and he would reply 'Not a lot, sometimes I wonder why I bother'. Later we would discuss this, mimicking and repeating what he had said, laughing. Well, there wasn't much entertainment in those days. Sadly he died in 2011; what memories I had when I attended the funeral.

Salisbury Fields

No story of Fordington would be complete without mention of Salisbury Fields, because this was our great playground. On one side of the field inside a 6-ft-high enclosure was the play equipment. Here we rode the swings and the roundabout – a May Pole-type arrangement with six chains hanging down with handles on the end. Clasping a handle, you ran around to get up speed, then lifted your feet up. The most exciting thing

Beyond this alley lies Salisbury Fields. We would rush through here to our 'field of dreams' where we played football ('I bags to be Stanley Matthews') and cricket ('I bags to be Dennis Compton'). Do children still use this phrase? It was much used when looking in toy shop windows at toys we could never hope to own.

was what we called the Jerker. It consisted of a long thick plank of wood hung on metal-hinged bars between two A frames made of scaffolding-type bars sunk into the ground. One of you stood at either end and you got it swinging back and forth. This item was so dangerous – in retrospect, it was like a huge swinging battering ram – but we loved it, and our aim, when older, was to get it swinging until it was as high as the fence, then, turning round, we leaped over the fence in what we called a parachute jump. Occasionally we turned an ankle, but never anything worse.

The rest of the field was used for cricket, football, rounders or any other game we might make up. Football was played with two coats thrown down as goal posts. Cricket was a dangerous game due to the uneven surface; the ball could suddenly rear up at all sorts of angles. It was quite normal to go home with a bruised cheek, loose tooth or split nose.

Once a year we would build a bonfire, and this was always huge, the biggest in Dorchester. For weeks before we would collect rubbish from around the town. We would borrow push trucks or barrows from one or

Salisbury Fields today, hardly changed from when we played here.

other of the stores and call on shops, collecting all their old cardboard and packing. We would also collect old and broken furniture from houses. Some of this furniture was often put inside the bonfire to form a camp. On one occasion the pile was the biggest anyone had ever seen, over 40 ft high; then one afternoon, a week before 5 November, disaster occurred. A fire engine and crew arrived and pulled it apart and burnt it, telling us it was too big to be safe. What disappointment.

In later years as teenagers, we all met up in Salisbury Fields. The girls were now of interest and we played records on the new invention, a portable record player that ran on a battery. One weird thing we did was to collect poppet beads; all the girls were wearing these at the time. They were plastic in many colours and snapped together to form a necklace. We would get one or two from each girl and form a long chain, the aim being to have one longer and more colourful than anyone else. We also amused ourselves with French knitting, seeing who could knit the longest tail of wool, sometimes 2 or 3 yards long.

The countryside around

As we grew older and were allowed further afield one of our great joys was to visit 'Pigeon Copse'. We would set off up Holloway Road, down the steps, across the river and quickly through Mill Street. Crossing London Road (with very little traffic) by Grey's Bridge we would enter the field. The river here was wide and reasonably deep on the road side of the hatches. This was the 'swimming baths' and in summer they received quite a lot of use. My mother would never let me swim there as she said I might catch polio. Was there any truth in that? Who knows? I think she just wanted to keep me out of the water.

The swimming baths just up from Grey's Bridge. On a summer's day crowds lay in the sun and bathed here in the cold fresh water of the Frome. (Copyright Mill Street Housing Society.)

Following the path on from here we would soon come to what we called 'Haunted House', a derelict cottage that had become overgrown. On our way we could never resist rummaging about here, looking for any little treasures that might reveal themselves. At the right time of year we picked apples and pears from trees in the garden; despite being grown over these still produced fruit, which to us, even when under-ripe, tasted delicious. Having finished our exploring we would journey on, crossing the track called Slyer's Lane (known as Lovers' Lane to us). Young couples looking for a quiet place frequented it, especially when the soldiers were in town. I often wonder how many children were conceived in this lane. Such a shame this is now a 'rat run'.

Slyer's Lane was once a quiet gravel track and idyllic spot. The squeals of delight sometimes heard told you that some of the young lovers enjoyed it very much.

Just the other side of the lane was a large chalk pit (now filled in). In this pit were some old mudguards from a lorry. We would carry these to the top of the pit and use them as toboggans. It's amazing how much fun we had with this. Moving on again we soon reached our objective, 'Pigeon Copse'. Here we would enjoy making bows and arrows from hazel wood. Eventually we became quite adept at this, and I am sure you would be surprised at the accuracy we could achieve.

On these trips we would often take a picnic – well, let's say a sandwich, not very grand. Occasionally we would have some lemonade, and this was homemade using 'Eiffel Tower'. This came in a blue box containing a blue glass bottle shaped like the Eiffel Tower, which was filled with powder a bit like sherbet. This powder was mixed with boiling water, then cooled and diluted. I expect today's children would turn their noses up at it, but to us it was just a bit special.

Bockhampton

Another of our visits to the countryside took us by the same route to Grey's Bridge, and then a hundred yards on the right to the path that leads to Bockhampton. The Dorchester bypass now crosses this once quiet country path. Before reaching Bockhampton, we passed the area around Stinsford and the lake at Kingston Maurward. We would cross the small stream and

enter the wooded area, which soon changed into a large clump of bamboo canes. We would cut ourselves one or two of these to use as spears. The lake was larger in those days, before it was dredged. There always seemed to be plenty of trout in the lake, although we did our best to relieve any overcrowding!

The area between the path known as Bockhampton Path to locals and the lake was covered in beautiful double snowdrops in spring; on occasions we would pick bunches for our mothers. There are some really tall trees bordering the path. We would climb high up into the branches until we were hidden by the foliage. From our vantage point we would await the arrival of walkers below, and would then make funny noises and amuse ourselves as people looked around trying to see where the noise had come from.

The River Frome, which takes many paths through and around Dorchester, is seen here near Stinsford, another of our favourite places.

Along the path you pass a track on the left leading to the old Elizabethan manor at Kingston Maurward. Often we would head up the lane to the house which was empty and in a state of disrepair. There was a barn owl that had set up home there and on occasions I collected owl pellets, which were taken to school and dissected to show all the small bones of voles and mice it had eaten. The house of course made a great playground; lots of places to hide in a game of hide and seek. On one occasion a lad (nameless) was hiding in the loft when his foot slipped off the beam and came through the ceiling. Impaling his leg on a nail on the way through, blood ran down, dripping onto the floor, which caused great hilarity. On other days some of us would remain in the house while the rest retreated down the lane to the bridge. From this area we would advance to attack the house, firing stones with catapults. Meanwhile those in the house attempted to defend it, firing stones from various windows. Looking back, this must have been a very dangerous pastime, it's a wonder someone didn't lose an eye.

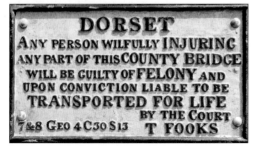

The River Frome was much deeper in the 1950s. Note the warning sign on Bockhampton Bridge and also the same on Grey's Bridge; no community service in those days.

Back on the path we headed for Bockhampton. Once there, we would check the river for fish and at the right time of year collect moorhen's eggs. These would be later carefully carried home and eaten. In modern times this must seem wrong; however, the moorhen's descendants are still seen in the same places at Bockhampton, so we can't have done much harm.

Bockhampton was just one big playground for us, and with the changing seasons there was always adventure of one sort or another to be had. I could write a book just on the times we had there. My pal Derek Pride lived at Bockhampton; his dad Alf was a great friend of ours, always ready to help us out of a scrape. He had bees and would give us lumps of honeycomb, which we would chew until the taste of honey was gone, then spit out the wax – wonderful! Also Alf grew Golden Drop gooseberries; these were a great favourite, so sweet and juicy. In our teens Alf made us two canoes. There was much more water in those days before they altered the course of the river, and we would race down from Minnow Bridge (halfway along the path leading to Stinsford), under Bockhampton Bridge, turn swiftly in the deep pool that lay on the right side of the bridge, out again and finish. Of course the odd accident was inevitable and we quite often got wet.

In season we collected sweet chestnuts at the rear of Stinsford churchyard, always wearing a pair of gloves to avoid the prickles. Bockhampton also provided large quantities of blackberries, and a good picking of these could always get you into mum's good books. Of course they were often a peace offering, required when we arrived home covered in black stains sustained when a blackberry war broke out.

Yellowham Woods

You may know these as Puddletown Forest or Thorncombe Wood, but to us they were 'Yellum Woods'. Here we built camps in the clumps of rhododendrons, and hung ropes from the branches of trees over the large dells that are a feature of these woods. The rope would allow us to swing out over the dell, making Tarzan cries. One of the games was to let go of the rope at full swing to see who could travel the farthest.

As I have said earlier, one of our hobbies was collecting birds' eggs. The one egg none of us had was a buzzard's. So it was that one sunny day in these woods we saw a buzzard leave its nest and circle high above the valley. The nest was at the very top of one of the tallest fir trees and it was decided that an attempt had to be made to collect one egg from the nest (we never took more than one from any nest). The duly elected member of our group started the long climb. From the start it was clear that the descent was going to be difficult. This was due to the fact that every small spar that was stepped on going up snapped off. Eventually, after great effort, the nest was reached. At that moment the buzzard realised what was happening and swooped down at the unfortunate robber. The egg was taken quickly and the robber, having placed the egg safely in his mouth, beat a rapid retreat down the tree. The first part of this journey through the branches was relatively simple. Then the part of the trunk with no grip was reached; the knobs left where the branches had snapped off slowed progress and the last 10 ft accelerated into a jump. As the lad landed hard on his heels, his mouth clamped shut and yolk ran from both corners of his mouth. The whole adventure had been a waste of time. Indeed, as far as I know, none of those involved ever did add a buzzard's egg to their collection.

While I am thinking about it, something comes to mind – this was all done wearing wellington boots. These were standard wear in all weathers, as were short trousers. How lucky modern children are. Oh, that sore red ring around your calf!

We also had an insatiable appetite for pets, so why not a pet squirrel? A squirrel would have to be young to accept you, we knew that much. Therefore it would need to come from the dray. These were located high in the pine trees in Yellum Woods, so another climb was called for. On this occasion I was elected to climb. As previously described, the ascent was not easy as the small branches broke off as I climbed. Having reached the desired height it was necessary to shin out along a branch to reach the dray. This was when the fun started. The young squirrels, feeling the vibrations, sensed danger and shot out along the branch, passing me hanging on for all I was worth. One, in his hurry, disappeared into my wellington boot. Realising its mistake, it rushed out again and took to the air, floated down and landed softly in the leaf mould under the tree. I was left holding on to the branch in a state of shock. Having landed, the squirrel was grabbed by those waiting below. I quickly gathered my senses and slithered down the tree, anxious to see the prize. But our new pet was far too wild to hold on to. Spitting, scratching and biting, it had escaped. Imagine the disappointment of having gone through all that, only to catch a fleeting glance of the squirrel as it flashed by.

To those who find some of our exploits cruel, I apologise. At our age and in those times it seemed natural and not in any way harsh. In our defence I can only say we were naturally inquisitive; however, we always treated animals with care and were never cruel to them.

And finally ...

These things are just a taste of what life was like for a Fordington boy in the post-war years. There are so many more tales I could tell but they may get a bit repetitive. When us lads (old men now) meet, as we do often, we discuss the old times and the fun we had; our wives get a little fed up seeing us still laughing about the same old things year after year. Times were hard then, we had little and there was little to be had. But we were happy with our lot and much more capable of entertaining ourselves than modern children, it seems. But I must stress that many of the things mentioned in this book are not recommended for children today in our safety conscious world.

Myself, David Moxom and Derek Pride at Spring Head Lake, still fishing together after too many years to mention.

I hope you have enjoyed this trawl through the past and thank you for purchasing this book. In doing so, you have helped two very worthwhile charities which I support.

Mill Street Housing Society

In 1905 Alfred Edwards, aged nineteen, started an interdenominational mission for the needs, spiritual and material, of Dorchester's poor. His base was an old thatched cottage beside the mill stream at the foot of the ridge dominated by Fordington's ancient parish church, St George's. The cottage lay in a network of alleys and lanes around a small square on a patch of low-lying ground. It was surrounded by the streams and ditches of the River Frome, crammed between the huge Duchy estate of Fordington Fields and the bounds of Dorchester town. The centre of a cholera epidemic in the 1850s, the clusters of damp and rotting houses of wattle and daub and cob were owned by small landlords who rented them by the room, with up to a dozen people of all ages occupying a single room. Thomas Hardy called the place Mixen Lane in *The Mayor of Casterbridge* and portrayed it as an isolated refuge of vagabonds and poachers living alongside the destitute and luckless.

Under the leadership of Alfred Edwards the Mill Street Mission gave away food and clothing, ran a bath house with hot water, held scripture readings, and taught girls sewing and cooking and boys scouting. In 1931 Alfred set up the Mill Street Housing Society, only the sixth such venture in the country. Florence, the widow of Thomas Hardy, became the first chairman, with Alfred as secretary, together with a committee of six. Well-wishers received share certificates for their subscriptions. The proceeds built the first three-bedroom homes, in Kings Road, for which the building contract stipulated that part of the workforce should be local. Florence Hardy laid the foundation stone in a ceremony watched by a good turnout of townsfolk and workmen.

More followed, with houses in Hardy Avenue, Holloway Road and Mill Street. A dilapidated old mill, Churchill's, a roller flour mill at the foot of the churchyard of St George's, was turned into flats with a shop in 1940. Two years later the society took over the neglected vicarage at the top of the hill. It had been a home well known by Thomas Hardy. The vicar's second son, Horace Moule, befriended young Hardy and introduced him to the company of university men and their families. Fordington Hill House now stands on its site. Millstream House was completed in 1964 and Edwards Court in 1993. The society's homes for ex-servicemen commemorate battles of the Second World War at which the county regiment, the Dorsets, formerly based at the Marabout Barracks near Top O'Town now called the Keep, were awarded medals.

Maurice Edwards, son of Alfred, took over the work in 1951 following his father's death. Rupert Edwards, the current chairman and grandson of the founder of the mission, carries the Mill Street Housing Society's work forward. The society continues to provide affordable housing in Fordington in the manner set out in 1931:

> 'to build houses or flats at the lowest possible rents. As is well known, there is still a great need for healthy accommodation among those who cannot afford the rent of the excellent houses provided by the Council. The Society will also endeavour to improve, where possible, any existing premises, if capable of acquisition on reasonable terms, and fit to be reconditioned. Where these are overcrowded, they can be re-let to smaller families, provided alternative accommodation is available for larger ones ... It is frankly admitted that the proposals may not be deemed to constitute a commercially attractive investment, but it is felt that there are sufficient people who are acutely aware of the evil effects of bad housing and who may be willing to thus assist in relieving this state of affairs.'

(Copyright Mill Street Housing Society.)

Other Roving Press Titles

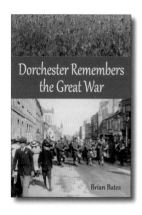

Dorchester Remembers the Great War

Brian Bates

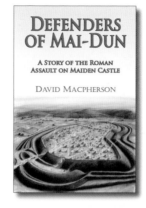

DEFENDERS OF MAI-DUN

A STORY OF THE ROMAN ASSAULT ON MAIDEN CASTLE

DAVID MACPHERSON

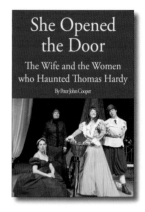

She Opened the Door

The Wife and the Women who Haunted Thomas Hardy

By Peter John Cooper

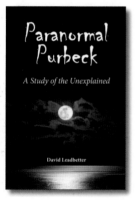

Paranormal Purbeck

A Study of the Unexplained

David Leadbetter

Discover Old Swanage

David Hayson

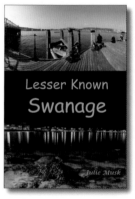

Lesser Known Swanage

Julie Musk

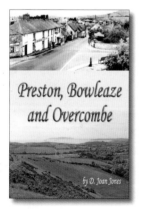

Preston, Bowleaze and Overcombe

by D. Joan Jones

The SPIRIT OF PORTLAND
Revelations of a Sacred Isle

Gary Biltcliffe

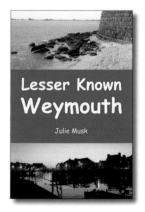

Lesser Known Weymouth

Julie Musk

If you like exploring, you'll love our books

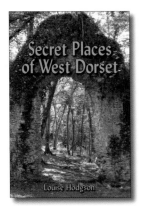

Secret Places of West Dorset
Louise Hodgson

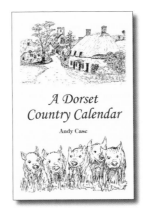

A Dorset Country Calendar
Andy Case

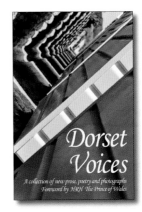

Dorset Voices
A collection of new prose, poetry and photographs
Foreword by HRH The Prince of Wales

THE PORTLAND CHRONICLES
THE PORTLAND SEA DRAGON
CAROL HUNT

Weymouth Bound
PAUL WESTON

THE PORTLAND CHRONICLES
ENCHANTMENT OF THE BLACK DOG
CAROL HUNT

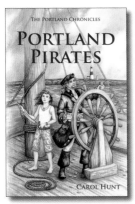

THE PORTLAND CHRONICLES
PORTLAND PIRATES
CAROL HUNT

Kids' Dorset

THE PORTLAND CHRONICLES
THE PORTLAND GIANT

Roving Press

www.rovingpress.co